Copyright No

Year of Publication -- 2014

Email -- manik85joshi@gmail.com

****

IMPORTANT NOTE

This Book is Part of a Series

SERIES Name: "English Daily Use"

[A Forty-Book Series]

BOOK Number: 16

BOOK Title: "English Grammar- Am, Is, Are, Was, Were"

****

Table of Contents

ENGLISH GRAMMAR- AM, IS, ARE, WAS, WERE

PATTERNS AND EXAMPLES

MANIK JOSHI

Dedication

THIS BOOK IS

DEDICATED

TO THOSE

WHO REALIZE

THE POWER OF ENGLISH

AND WANT TO

LEARN IT

SINCERELY

Verb 'To Be'

The Verb **'to be'** is used to represent the following English verbs:

'Am', 'Is', 'Are' [Present Tense] **|** **'Was', 'Were'** [Past Tense]

Following are also the forms of the verb 'to be':

to be *[Infinitive]*

being *[Present Participle]*

been *[Past Participle]*

be *[Present Subjunctive]*

were *[Past Subjunctive]*

be *[Imperative]*

The verb **'to be'** is used as both a ***linking verb*** and **an *auxiliary verb***.

LINKING VERB:

A verb that connects a subject with the complement (adjective or noun) that describes it.

Example: He is an engineer. [In this sentence, the subject (he) and noun (engineer) are connected by **linking verb 'is'**.]

Some more examples:

I **am** happy. [linking verb – am]

Is he a good boy? [linking verb – is]

We **are** very proud of ourselves. [linking verb – are]

She **was** intelligent. [linking verb – was]

They **were** not late by half an hour. [linking verb – were]

AUXILIARY VERB:

A verb that conjoins with the **main verb** to show tenses, etc.

Example: He is going to the office. [In this sentence, the -ing form of the **main verb 'go'** has been used with the **auxiliary verb 'is'**.

Some more examples:

I **am studying** a book. [auxiliary verb – am | main verb – study (-ing form)]

He **is working** on his project [auxiliary verb – is | main verb – work (-ing form)]

We **are** not **expected** to tell the secret. [auxiliary verb – are | main verb – expect (past participle form)]

She **was taught** by me. [auxiliary verb – was | main verb – teach (past participle form)]

Were they **burdened** by high taxation [auxiliary verb – were | main verb – burden (past participle form)]

IMPORTANT POINTS ABOUT THE VERB 'TO BE'

'AM' –

Singular Verb

Used In Present Tense

Used with Subject 'I'

'IS' –

Singular Verb

Used In Present Tense

Used with Subject 'He' 'She', 'It' and other Singular Subjects

'ARE' –

Plural Verb

Used In Present Tense

Used with Subject 'We', 'You', 'They' and other Plural Subjects

'WAS' –

Singular Verb

Used In Past Tense

Used with Subject 'I', 'He', She', 'It' and other Singular Subjects

'WERE' –

Plural Verb

Used In Past Tense

Used with Subject 'We', 'You' and other Plural Subjects

Verb 'To Be' -- Negative Patterns

The negative form of the ***verb 'to be'*** *can be made by adding* ***'not'*** *after the* ***verb 'to be'***.

Examples:

I **am not** worried about the financial loss.

He **is not** worried about the financial loss.

She **is not** worried about the financial loss.

You **are not** worried about the financial loss.

We **are not** worried about the financial loss.

They **are not** worried about the financial loss.

I **was not** worried about the financial loss.

He **was not** worried about the financial loss.

She **was not** worried about the financial loss.

You **were not** worried about the financial loss.

We **were not** worried about the financial loss.

They **were not** worried about the financial loss.

CONTRACTION – ['TO BE' + 'NOT']

Am – am not [Amn't] (Use of this contraction is Outdated)

Is – Is not [Isn't]

Are – Are not [Aren't]

Was – Was not [Wasn't]

Were – Were not [Weren't]

Examples:

He **isn't** worried about the financial loss.

She **isn't** worried about the financial loss.

You **aren't** worried about the financial loss.

We **aren't** worried about the financial loss.

They **aren't** worried about the financial loss.

I **wasn't** worried about the financial loss.

He **wasn't** worried about the financial loss.

She **wasn't** worried about the financial loss.

You **weren't** worried about the financial loss.

We **weren't** worried about the financial loss.

They **weren't** worried about the financial loss.

CONTRACTION - ['SUBJECT' + 'TO BE']

You can also use the short form of **'subject' + 'to be'**

I + am = I'm

He + is = He's

She + is = She's

You + are = You're

We + are = We're

They + are = They're

It + is = It's

Note: *There is no short form of 'Subject + Was' and 'Subject + Were'*

Examples:

I'm not worried about the financial loss.

He's not worried about the financial loss.

She's not worried about the financial loss.

You're not worried about the financial loss.

We're not worried about the financial loss.

They're not worried about the financial loss.

Verb 'To Be' -- Interrogative Patterns

The interrogative form of the **verb 'to be'** *can be made by putting* the **verb 'to be'** *before the* ***subject.***

Examples:

Am *I* comfortable with such functions?

Is *he* comfortable with such functions?

Is *she* comfortable with such functions?

Are *you* comfortable with such functions?

Are *they* comfortable with such functions?

Are *we* comfortable with such functions?

Was *I* comfortable with such functions?

Was *he* comfortable with such functions?

Was *she* comfortable with such functions?

Were *you* comfortable with such functions?

Were *they* comfortable with such functions?

Were we comfortable with such functions?

VERB 'TO BE' -- INTERROGATIVE-NEGATIVE PATTERNS

The interrogative-negative form of the **verb 'to be'** *can be made by putting* ***'not' after the subject*** *and using* the **verb 'to be'** *before the* ***subject.***

Examples:

Am *I* **not** comfortable with such functions?

Is *he* **not** comfortable with such functions?

Is *she* **not** comfortable with such functions?

Are *you **not*** comfortable with such functions?

Are *they* **not** comfortable with such functions?

Are *we* **not** comfortable with such functions?

Was *I* **not** comfortable with such functions?

Was *he* **not** comfortable with such functions?

Was *she* **not** comfortable with such functions?

Were *you* **not** comfortable with such functions?

Were *they* **not** comfortable with such functions?

Were we **not** comfortable with such functions?

CONTRACTION – ['TO BE' + 'NOT']

In interrogative-negative sentences, the **contraction** of **'to be' + 'not'** is used before the subject.

Examples:

Isn't *he* comfortable with such functions?

Isn't *she* comfortable with such functions?

Aren't *you* comfortable with such functions?

Aren't *they* comfortable with such functions?

Aren't *we* comfortable with such functions?

Wasn't *I* comfortable with such functions?

Wasn't *he* comfortable with such functions?

Wasn't *she* comfortable with such functions?

Weren't *you* comfortable with such functions?

Weren't *they* comfortable with such functions?

Weren't we comfortable with such functions?

NOTE: Contraction of "Am not"

For the subject "*I*" there is no contraction of "am + not". To say "Amn't I" is not proper because the use of the contraction amn't is outdated. Instead, you should use "**Aren't I**".

Aren't I not comfortable with such functions?

The use of "Aren't I" is common in informal communication, but in formal English, you should prefer using "Am I Not".

INTERROGATIVE SENTENCES WITH QUESTION WORDS

Use 'Question Word' before the ***verb 'to be'*** *+ Subject.*

Pattern:

Question Word + 'Be' + Subject

List of Question (or Interrogative) words and what they imply:

What – implies 'specific information' or confirmation/repetition

When – implies 'at what time' or 'on what occasion'

Where – implies 'in what place, position or situation'

Which – implies 'choice or alternative'

Who – implies 'identity' of a subject (person/people)

Whom – implies 'identity' of an object (person/people)

Whose – implies 'who something belongs to'

Why – implies 'reason, explanation or purpose'

How – implies 'way or manner', 'condition or quality'

Examples:

***What* are** your students actually **learning?**

***When* are** you **leaving** this place?

***Where* are** all of these people **coming** from?

***Which* are** the best cities for tourists?

***Who* were** the top scorers in England's top four football leagues last year?

***Whose* is** the other bag?

***Why* is** she **coming** late?

***How* are** they **changing** the workplace?

'TO BE' SHORT ANSWERS

Affirmative and negative short answers to questions --

Pattern for Short Affirmative Answer --

Yes + pronoun + verb to be

Pattern for Short Negative Answer --

No + pronoun + verb to be + not (n't)

Example –

Question: Is *he* comfortable with such functions?

Complete Affirmative Answer: **Yes,** he is comfortable with such functions.

Short Affirmative answer: **Yes, he is.**

Complete Negative Answer: **No,** he is not comfortable with such functions.

Short Negative answer: **No, he is not. [No, he isn't / No, he's not]**

NOTE –

Contraction of 'Subject' + 'To Be' is not used in Affirmative Short Answers. In the above example, you cannot write – Yes, he's. You must write **– Yes, he is.**

Obviously, you can write - Yes, he's comfortable with such functions.

ALSO, NOTE- "as/that was" [phrase of 'be']

Meaning: as someone or something was previously called; formerly

"as/that was" is used after a former name –

Iran— Persia as was.

Myanmar— Burma as was.

Thailand— Siam as was.

Russia— the Soviet Union as was.

1A. English Grammar – 'Am'

English Verb 'AM' Represents Present Events.

It Is 'Singular' In Sense.

It Is Strictly Used With the Subject "I".

EXAMPLES:

AFFIRMATIVE SENTENCES

I **am** deep in my studies.

I **am** perfectly at home.

I **am** proud to have a consistent progressive record of leadership.

I **am** sick and tired but I wish them well.

I **am** very grateful to the president for welcoming me so warmly.

NEGATIVE SENTENCES

I **am not** a robot.

I **am not** aware of the risk of living here.

INTERROGATIVE SENTENCES

Am I answerable to the public?

Am I not **attractive** enough?

Am I **not** under debt?

INTERROGATIVE SENTENCES [With Question Words]

***How* am** I not your friend?

***Where* am** I now?

***Where* am** I supposed to go to?'

***How* am** I supposed to live without you?

1B. AM + -ING Form of Verb

"Present Continuous Tense"

Expresses **-** Continued Action In Present

EXAMPLES:

AFFIRMATIVE SENTENCES

I **am driving** at a moderate speed of 40 miles per hour.

I **am running** to keep myself fit.

I **am studying** my notes.

I **am writing** a book.

NEGATIVE SENTENCES

I **am not drawing** a portrait.

I **am not practicing** daily for the function.

INTERROGATIVE SENTENCES

Am I **facing** uncertainty?

Am I **asking** the right questions?

Am I **not working** on my new project?

INTERROGATIVE SENTENCES [With Question Words]

When **am** I **going** to be back?

Which of her needs **am** I **not meeting?**

Why **am** I **not losing** weight?

I'm practicing – so ***why*** **am** I **not getting** better?

How **am** I really **doing** compared with others my age?

1C. AM + Being + Past Participle

"Present Continuous Tense – Passive Voice"

EXAMPLES:

AFFIRMATIVE SENTENCES

I **am being awarded** for my excellent work.

I **am being expected** to win a trophy.

I **am being greeted** by my family members.

I **am being inundated** with calls from various people.

I **am being made** a scapegoat

I **am being targeted** in a decade-old case.

I **am being taught** computer programming by my teacher.

I **am being treated** like I'm not a part of this country.

NEGATIVE SENTENCES

I **am not being asked** to leave a country.

I **am not being given** a lot of work.

INTERROGATIVE SENTENCES

Am I **being persecuted** for my activism?

Am I **being placed** in the top category?

Am I **not being chased** by someone?

INTERROGATIVE SENTENCES [With Question Words]

***Why* am** I **being double-charged**?

***Why* am** I **being dragged** into this controversy?

***Why* am** I **being forced** to get married?

***Why* am** I **being placed** under house arrest?

1D. AM + Past Participle

"Present Indefinite Tense – Passive Voice"

EXAMPLES:

AFFIRMATIVE SENTENCES

I **am asked** to finish his tasks.

I **am given** breakfast by my wife.

I **am sent** a birthday gift every year by my son.

NEGATIVE SENTENCES

I **am not accompanied** by my colleagues at the office.

I **am not advised** not to go out at night.

INTERROGATIVE SENTENCES

Am I **not called** by him every morning?

Am I **not told** about his health conditions often?

INTERROGATIVE SENTENCES [With Question Words]

Why **am** I **asked** to defend my choice on a regular basis?

Why **am** I **expected** to endure harassment?

Why **am** I **told** to act like an adult?

2A. English Grammar – 'Is'

English Verb 'IS' Represents Present Events.

It Is 'Singular' In Sense.

It Is Used With 'He', 'She', 'It' and all 'Singular' Subjects.

EXAMPLES:

AFFIRMATIVE SENTENCES

A long-term plan **is** very difficult for young people.

A rainy day in summer **is** a great blessing.

A relief operation **is** in progress.

Arming rebels **is** a dangerous decision.

Avoid doing what you know **is** wrong.

Conducting mock drills in schools and industries **is** a regular exercise.

Cracked lips during winter **is** a widespread problem.

Cycling **is** a good exercise for remaining healthy and fit.

Education for most children in slum areas **is** a far-sighted dream.

Everybody **is** equally happy here.

Everyone **is** equally responsible for it.

Everyone **is** scared.

The fitness of police personnel **is** imperative given the nature of the job.

Hard work **is** the key to success.

He **is** 10 days short of his 50th birthday.

He **is** a pensioner now.

He **is** glad to be back here now.

He **is** in mounting trouble due to a spate of police complaints.

He **is** lucky enough to have a small house with a rather modest rent.

He **is** notorious for comments often deemed offensive.

He **is** on leave for introspection.

His action **is** an outcome of his frustration of losing the election.

His ailment **is** "much better".

His aim **is** admirable and realistic.

His firstborn **is** a girl.

His huge debt **is** the legacy of the past.

His post **is** largely ceremonial.

Home **is** the hospital, and the world outside **is** a battlefield.

Horror **is** still writ large on his face.

India **is** in a very tough and fragile neighborhood.

It **is** a preventive measure and as well as prohibitive and punitive.

It **is** a top spot that both Germany and France don't want.

It **is** an altogether different story.

It **is** energy that makes things work.

It **is** high noon.

It **is** highly likely.

It **is** impossible to re-conduct the exam within the time frame decided by the court.

It **is** like a dream.

It **is** our fate to face this.

It **is** over a month since that incident.

It **is** the creation of the media.

It **is** too early to say anything at this stage.

It **is** an unending stream of visitors.

It **is** way beyond what I imagined.

The missile **is** a rocket-propelled weapon.

The monitoring system **is** weak.

My name **is** close to the name of my friend.

My neighbor **is** like a member of our family.

My statement **is** open to interpretation.

My stature **is** too big for such roles.

Nowadays litigation **is** on the increase.

Online procedure **is** both convenient and a time-saver.

Our country **is** a coming great power.

Our organization **is** back on its wheels now.

Public safety **is** of prime importance.

The radiation leak **is** bigger than thought.

The road **is** nowhere near completion.

Saturday **is** the day off.

Slowing growth **is** the 'most worrisome' factor.

Soil testing **is** the most essential tool to diagnose the physical, chemical and biological properties of soil.

Sowing **is** on in the northeastern states.

Staying in Everest **is** impossible.

Such apathetic and insensitive behavior from him **is** very unfortunate.

Teaching **is** what I do best.

That **is** what you always say.

The advisory **is** effective till further order.

The choice **is** between his duty and religion.

The Governor **is** out on a tour.

The number of women joining the campaign **is** constantly on the rise.

The ornament of the night **is** the moon.

The pace of work at present **is** likely to stay this way till Wednesday.

The problem **is** two-fold.

The situation **is** unlikely to change in at least the next four-five days.

The whole day's journey **is** quite tiring.

Their target **is** to cut down line-loss to 10% from its present 24%.

This bark **is** chewable.

This **is** an example of his double speak.

This **is** only a test.

This **is** quite right.

This **is** the craziest thing you've done.

This **is** the rest period in home loan offers.

This **is** the second success that I have achieved.

This **is** your daily routine.

This matter **is** still in the discussion stage.

This shirt **is** loose at the waist.

Providing them with the best possible treatment **is** our top priority.

Tobacco use in any form **is** a well-established cause of cancers in the mouth, food pipe and lungs.

Traveling without a ticket **is** a serious crime.

The use of mosquito nets **is** very effective in preventing malaria.

What you have seen **is** only the start.

Whatever he has been accused of doing **is** purely a personal matter.

Wheat **is** a cash crop.

When ease **is** disturbed, it **is** 'dis-ease'.

NEGATIVE SENTENCES

The decline in poverty **is not** real and encouraging.

Democracy **is not** just about holding elections at periodic intervals.

Fever **is not** always dengue.

He **is not** blind in one eye.

He **is not** into fasting.

His promotion **is not** my concern.

It **is not** a cruel joke.

It **is not** a handheld device.

It **is not** a pleasant trip.

It **is not** a step in the right direction.

It **is not** appropriate to say something about the issue when the investigation is on.

It **is not** dirty.

It **is not** easy to import.

It **is not** a proven fact.

It **is not** right for a responsible person like me to comment at this stage.

It **is not** the first time that crops have failed because of untimely rain.

Let alone other amenities, there **is not** even a proper visitor's path here.

Money **is not** an issue when it comes to health.

The new bus station **is not** far away from the present location.

The summer paddy crop **is not** ready for harvesting in many parts of the country.

This case **is not** "such a big one"

This committee **is not** a Statutory Body.

This house **is not** habitable.

This **is not** improper pressure.

This **is not** the best song ever.

This **is not** the true purpose of our lives.

This mango **is not** overripe.

This village certainly **is not** impressed with one year of his rule.

INTERROGATIVE SENTENCES

Is he lame in one leg/foot?

Is he our tallest leader?

Is his mother a homemaker?

Is the medical profession very unpredictable?

Is physical disability a hindrance to excellence?

Is she averse to this idea?

Is the long jump a lot more difficult than a sprint?

Is the project still far from completion?

Is the status of education **v**ery poor here?

Is this a clear departure from tradition?

Is this an indication of the gravity of the problem?

Is this the biggest misconception he has about life?

Is this the way they are bringing us good days?

Is this **not** the latest career trend?

Is this **not** the true purpose of our lives?

INTERROGATIVE SENTENCES [With Question Words]

Why **is** he so afraid of competition?

Why **is** health care so damn expensive?

Why **is** paperless finance important?

Why **is** there so much debt?

How **is** Ethereum different from Bitcoin?

2B. IS + -ING Form of Verb

"Present Continuous Tense"

Expresses **-** Continued Action In Present

EXAMPLES:

AFFIRMATIVE SENTENCES:

A question mark **is hovering** over the fate of the interstate tennis championship to be held next year.

The army **is** currently **working** to restore the damaged road.

Asia's rise **is gathering** pace.

The city **is reeling** under tiger scare again.

Everyone **is trying** to contact each other.

He **is aging**.

He **is breathing** spontaneously.

He **is bridging** the gap between two major parties of the country.

He **is carrying** a laptop into his office.

The investigating officer **is appealing** to the public for more information

The newspaper **is withholding** the names of the victims.

Police **are probing** the possibility of an organized racket behind the alleged fake degrees of students.

The river **is dipping** steadily.

She **is competing** with others for a $10,000 grand prize.

The awareness **is seeping** into the region.

The bubble **is bursting.**

The cow **is chewing** chaff from the feed bin.

The tiger population **is falling** across the world, it **is rising** in India.

This incident **is drawing** the attention of the entire country.

Vegetarian food **is catching** up as a global trend due to its health benefits.

NEGATIVE SENTENCES

He **is not betting** on the match.

He **is not playing** by the rules.

I want him to speak on this but he **is not doing** so.

INTERROGATIVE SENTENCES

Is the situation **returning** to normal?

Is the violence in the state **not plumbing** new depths?

INTERROGATIVE SENTENCES [With Question Words]

Why **is** he **doing** that?

***Why* is** opinion **growing** against the management's decision?

2C. IS + Being + Past Participle

"Present Continuous Tense – Passive Voice"

EXAMPLES:

AFFIRMATIVE SENTENCES

A lot of good work **is being done.**

A sheet **is being spread** for the children to sit on.

An attempt **is being made** to stifle his voice.

The City council **is being asked** to approve a review of the existing shelter system.

The coal supply **is being cleared** by the government.

Every panel **is being planned**.

Food **is being cooked.**

He **is being held** against his will.

He says he **is being** wrongly **defamed.**

His business **is being** poorly **managed.**

His murder **is being given** the shape of a suicide.

In several areas, contaminated water **is being supplied**.

It **is being seen** as a move loaded with political significance.

It **is** now **being tested**.

The National Register of Citizens **is being updated.**

Our company **is being reorganized.**

Saving people **is being put** first.

Such a plan **is** perhaps **being tried** out for the first time in the country.

The proposal for a new bus stand **is being made** considering the heavy rush at the present stands.

NEGATIVE SENTENCES

He **is not being punished**.

My house **is not being renovated**.

The matter **is not being investigated**.

INTERROGATIVE SENTENCES:

Is the computer **being repaired** by the engineer?

Is he **being called** a superstar?

Is the letter **not being written** to the higher authorities?

INTERROGATIVE SENTENCES [With Question Words]

Why **is** he **being released?**

Why **is** he **being singled out?**

How **is** education **being disrupted** by technology?

2D. IS + Past Participle

"Present Indefinite Tense – Passive Voice"

EXAMPLES:

AFFIRMATIVE SENTENCES

A narrow distance **is left** to reach the boy.

Being a heritage city, no one **is allowed** to build houses here their own way.

Drinking lots of water and consumption of seasonal fruits **is advised** to beat heat strokes.

Ensure that no one **is** falsely **framed**.

It is time he **is controlled.**

The main road to the city **is riddled** with gaping holes.

NEGATIVE SENTENCES

He **is not known** for talking nonsense.

She **is not known** to speak her heart out about issues.

INTERROGATIVE SENTENCES:

Is he **known** for his propriety and credibility?

Is tying threads **not considered** to be wish-fulfilling?

INTERROGATIVE SENTENCES [With Question Words]

***Why* is** he **accused** of 'causing disappearance of evidence?'

***How* is** real estate commission **affected** if you find a home yourself?

***How* is** the mental illness **treated?**

3A. English Grammar – 'Are'

English Verb 'ARE' Represents Present Events.

It Is 'Plural' In a Sense.

It Is Used With 'You', 'We', 'They', and all 'Plural' Subjects.

EXAMPLES:

AFFIRMATIVE SENTENCES

A majority of fire hydrants in the city **are** nonfunctional.

A number of plans **are** in the pipeline to give a major face-lift to the region.

All sensitive examination centers **are** under the scanner.

The best years **are** yet to come.

Dogs **are** somewhat like young human children.

Efforts **are** on to trace four of their accomplices.

For every 10 tigers, there **are** 9 goats.

Give it up if you **are** afraid.

Government guidelines **are** the same for every recruitment center.

He knows who his enemies **are** now.

Her wages **are** low.

His days **are** "numbered," rather than "over."

His father and mother **are** teachers in a government school.

Horses **are** four million years old.

Infiltration patterns **are** in consonance with previous years.

Investigations **are** under process while other miscreants are yet to be nabbed.

Lit-up garbage heaps **are** a common sight in this colony.

Many cases **are** under intense public scrutiny.

Many items of historical importance **are** present here.

Many parents **are** in constant worry for their children's safety.

Medical facilities **are** grossly inadequate due to the absence of a health care center in the village.

Most drug addicts **are** under 25.

A number of kids **are** internet addicts.

Of the city's 1 million people 0.5 million **are** English-speaking settlers.

Pain-relieving balms **are** difficult to ban considering their household utility in everyday life.

Police **are** on the lookout for him.

Residents **are** now hopeful for the improvement of the situation.

Spiking home prices **are** a cause for concern.

Sunflowers **are** a little different from crops like corn or cotton.

The days **are** long, but the nights **are** short.

These **are** eventful times.

These **are** just two questions of many we answered today.

These **are** people that all of us like.

These areas **are** like black holes.

They **are** one on the issue.

Tigers **are** territorial animals.

Twelve others **are** also in the fray.

US consumers feel more confident but **are** still cautious.

We **are** all a mix of good and bad energies.

We **are** happy that we succeeded in our efforts.

We **are** hopeful of an early solution to the issues.

We **are** ready to make all sacrifices for this battle.

We **are** so close to the end.

We increased the number of buses, which **are** 60 at present to 80.

Women **are** present in all walks of life.

You **are** more a problem than a solution.

NEGATIVE SENTENCES

Manage your time so that you **are not** in a hurry.

They **are not** from the teaching fraternity.

Tiger visits **are not** common in the city.

We **are not** inferior to any other country.

INTERROGATIVE SENTENCES

Are animals useful in children's books?

Are education and success synonymous?

Are his chances of survival slim?

Are investigations underway?

Are leadership and learning indispensable to each other?

Are many women afraid of stepping out?

Are museums vulnerable to vandalism?

Are people who work a lot much more prone to be short-sleepers?

Are self-disciplined people happier?

Are stadiums full beyond capacity?

Are two-reactor sites **not** near each other?

INTERROGATIVE SENTENCES [With Question Words]

Why **are** leaves green?

Why **are** so many college graduates jobless?

Why **are** the letters of the alphabet in that order?

Why **are** we so vulnerable to crime online?

Timber-framed vs traditional houses – **which are** better?

3B. ARE + -ING Form of Verb

"Present Continuous Tense"

Expresses - Continued Action In Present

EXAMPLES:

AFFIRMATIVE SENTENCES

Both the child and the mother **are doing** fine.

Checking squads **are operating** in full swing.

Critics of our proposal **are multiplying**.

In everything we do, we **are** always **consulting** with each other.

Now you **are seeing** just the reverse.

Our relatives **are** now constantly **questioning** us about the incident.

Police **are** currently **interrogating** people in the neighborhood.

Police **are probing** different angles of the crime.

Police teams **are raiding** his suspected hideouts.

Police teams **are scrutinizing** voluminous documents seized during raids on different premises owned by them.

Preparations **are going** on at breakneck speed.

Property taxes **are going up.**

Railway authorities **are figuring out** how to keep stray animals away from the semi-high speed train's tracks.

Road accident victims **are battling** for their lives in hospitals.

Some states **are doing** well; others **are lagging** behind.

Standards in all higher exams **are falling**!

The good news is that fewer people **are using** drugs in our city.

The things they **are proposing** to do are a complete violation of users' privacy.

They **are bringing** new technology to the farmers.

They **are grieving**.

Water bodies **are dying** a slow death due to encroachment.

We **are** closely **monitoring** the situation.

We **are going** after them wherever they are, with everything that we have.

We **are issuing** a fresh notification.

We **are striving** to achieve our goal in the coming 15 months.

We **are waiting** to see his performance.

We **are witnessing** the shrinkage of land available for agriculture.

You, with all due respect, **are floating** too high.

NEGATIVE SENTENCES

Despite talk of job creation, young people **are not finding** job opportunities.

The rivers in the region **are not overflowing**.

They **are not treating** the incident as terror-related.

Today, heart diseases **are *no longer* discriminating** between the young and old. [Note: use of 'no longer' instead of not]

We **are not asking** for it as a favor but as "right".

We **are not begging** for alms.

INTERROGATIVE SENTENCES

Are Industries **dirtying** the water bodies?

Are Investors **making** serious mistakes in the market?

Are states **reeling** under a power crisis?

Are they fast **expanding** their areas of influence?

Are we **not proceeding** with caution?

Are youths **not building** the country they desire?

INTERROGATIVE SENTENCES [With Question Words]

***Why* are** gold prices **rising?**

***Why* are** people **taking** to the streets?

***Why* are** some businesses **charging** extra for card payments?

***Why* are** you **leaving** your job?

3C. ARE + Being + Past Participle

"Present Continuous Tense – Passive Voice"

EXAMPLES:

AFFIRMATIVE SENTENCES

All safety norms **are being followed** by employees of the department be it regular or contractual staff.

All those people relevant to the case **are being examined**.

Applications **are being accepted** online.

Auditions **are being held.**

Billions **are being spent** on global warming measures.

Bushes and trees **are being pruned**.

The consequences of declining paddy prices **are being felt** by farmers.

Enhancements **are being mounted** properly.

Family members **are being cautioned** to stay alert and comfort patients if they see signs of distress.

Flags **are being flown** at half-mast.

Positive steps **are being taken** to ensure a brighter future for all of us.

Such programs **are being held** throughout the state.

The injured **are being air-transported**.

These buildings **are being built** in medieval style.

They **are being forced** to live in horrible conditions.

They **are being treated** fairly and are all well.

We **are being treated** as an enemy by them.

You should approach the nodal body if you **are being threatened**.

NEGATIVE SENTENCES

His achievements **are not being highlighted**.

People **are not being invited** to have their say on proposed changes to the law.

We **aren't being paid** or **given** adequate food.

INTERROGATIVE SENTENCES

Are houses **being refurbished?**

Are important decisions **being taken**?

Are students' library concerns **being ignored**?

Are they **not being insulted** by the actions of their son?

INTERROGATIVE SENTENCES [With Question Words]

Why **are** papers **being wasted** in the office?

Why **are** they **not being sheltered?**

3D. ARE + Past Participle

"Present Indefinite Tense – Passive Voice"

EXAMPLES:

AFFIRMATIVE SENTENCES

A bundle of TV shows **is launched** every now and then.

Children **are considered** to be pure and true at heart.

Failures **are followed** by successes.

In Urdu, figures **are written** left to right, even though the script is read right to left.

Market data and analytics **are derived** from primary and secondary research.

New companies **are granted** tax breaks.

Party leaders **are** simply **silenced** for reaction.

They **are known** to work with military precision.

They **are respected** the world over.

Today's verdicts **are expected** to provide the much-needed ammunition to the Opposition party.

Today's school-leavers **are confronted** with more than 1,000 courses.

Traders **are given** a yearly contract by the Municipal Corporation to put up hoardings and flexes.

Villagers **are allowed** to bring fodder for their cattle from the field.

When common salts **are dissolved** in water, a 'shell' of water molecules is formed around them.

NEGATIVE SENTENCES

A genius **is not born** but made.

Relationships **are not developed** merely by talking, but by nurturing them.

Teams have been dispatched so that the idols **are not exported**.

We **are not trained** to effectively tackle natural disaster-like situations.

INTERROGATIVE SENTENCES

Are drinking water pipes **disrupted**?

Are they **not entrusted** with the task of evaluating around 10 million answer copies?

INTERROGATIVE SENTENCES [With Question Words]

***Why* are** women **accused** of witchcraft?

***How* are** cases **filed** in courts?

***How* are** rooms **cleaned** at an ice hotel?

***How* are** you **perceived** at work?

4A. English Grammar – 'Was'

English Verb 'WAS' Represents Past Events.

It Is 'Singular' In Sense.

It Is Used With 'He', 'She', 'It' and all 'Singular' Subjects

EXAMPLES:

AFFIRMATIVE SENTENCES

A surprise inspection by the district magistrate revealed that the science center **was** in a deplorable state.

All he could do **was** watch.

He claimed that the city **was** under an undeclared curfew.

He gave the impression that he **was** eager.

He **was** a substitute help.

He **was** apparently in a state of depression.

He **was** the epitome of the highest human ideal conduct.

He **was** an expert in fitting pipelines.

He **was** handicapped and moved with the help of crutches.

He **was** in deep slumber after completing household chores.

He **was** in no condition to speak.

He **was** into education, hotel and real estate business.

He **was** the kind of job candidate that every hiring manager wanted on his team.

He **was** on his way back home after his night duty.

He **was** only partly responsible for the mishap.

He **was** a part-time activist.

He **was** very much familiar with the city.

He **was** yet to receive his resignation.

His motive behind passing baseless remarks **was** to break the unity among citizens.

His sentence **was** a reduction in rank and forfeiture of $500 in pay.

I **was** in an extremely defenseless position.

It **was** a nightmare in daylight.

It **was** a shock for me.

It **was** a strange night.

It **was** a very disturbing development.

It **was** close to sunset.

It **was** much above the required number of 100.

It **was** not a made-up story.

It **was** only when the media got wind of the crime on April 12 that the police lodged a complaint.

It **was** so disgraceful to train somebody else to take over your job.

It **was** still a matter of speculation.

It **was** time for me to move on.

Life **was** good.

Loneliness **was** my fortune of creation.

My condition **was** similar.

My desire **was** to break the world record.

Organ donation pledge **was** their only wedding gift.

Polling **was** largely peaceful.

She **was** full of life.

That day like this year **was** a Sunday.

That Incident **was** ‘incredibly concerning”.

That, in effect, **was** that.

The ad **was** for a good cause with a noble intention.

The air **was** thick with a foul smell.

The door **was** low.

The economy of the country **was** in poor shape.

The gunbattle **was** on till late afternoon.

The incident **was** the fallout of an old rivalry.

The infection **was** too much for the body to handle.

The last outbreak year **was** 2003.

The national anthem **was** on.

The picture the boy painted **was** really horrific.

The place **was** scenic.

The plane **was** mid-air.

The safety latch **was** in place.

The survey **was** a part of an academic exercise.

There **was** a ruckus in school after the teacher cut students' hair.

This **was** sometime in 2001.

Traffic on the road **was** thin.

The TV channel **was** in the air.

What she did **was** unwarranted.

Whatever she did **was** a good intention.

Work of concretizing the pavement **was** on.

NEGATIVE SENTENCES

He **was not** in a proper frame of mind.

He **was not** in a transferrable job.

He **was not** reckless with money.

It **was not** a fit case for a grant of divorce.

It **was not** ridiculous.

The notification **was not** in violation of the Constitution.

She **was not** someone who could commit suicide.

The design of the bombs **was not** faulty.

The night **was not** a calm one.

The road **was not** narrow.

What he did **was not** criminal.

What she did **was not** extraordinary.

INTERROGATIVE SENTENCES

Was he also into sports?

Was he at the center of controversy?

Was he hopeful of his victory?

Was it a productive meeting?

Was it an anonymous call?

Was it a bid to rouse passions?

Was life hell for him?

Was the office short of staff?

Was she unable to conceive children?

Was the protest **not** peaceful?

INTERROGATIVE SENTENCES [With Question Words]

Why **was** he in such a bad mood?

Why **was** there a series of power cuts across the state on Sunday night?

How **was** your first day of classes?

How **was** your relationship with him?

How **was** your weekend?

4B. WAS + -ING Form of Verb

"Past Continuous Tense"

Expresses **-** Continued Action In the Past

EXAMPLES:

AFFIRMATIVE SENTENCES

A train **was speeding** his way, as he **was talking** on his cell phone.

The airline **was grappling** with a funds crunch and an aging fleet.

The baby **was flailing** her arms and legs.

The building **was leaning** dangerously.

The evening **was approaching**.

He **was ailing** for some time.

He **was battling** for life after she ate a poison substance under an apparent suicide pact.

He **was driving** under the influence of alcohol.

He **was heading** a new provisional government.

He **was pacing** the floor.

He **was** pillion **riding** on a bike.

He **was playing** with five of his friends in front of his house.

He **was** profusely **bleeding**.

He **was reaching** the limits of his patience.

He **was sleeping** at his home without shutting the doors.

He **was staking** a claim for being the tallest family in records.

He **was working out** ways to break off the alliance!

The heavy presence of police in the area **was instilling** fear among locals, rather than confidence.

His body had injury marks and his head **was bleeding**.

His voice **was breaking** in pain because of the burns on his body.

I thought he **was losing** his head.

I **was tossing** in my bed.

I **was trying** to write the best book I could.

The investigating agency **was following** procedure.

The officer said he **was awaiting** the postmortem report.

She **was coping** with the double blow of her husband's arrest and his son's heart attack.

She **was standing** close to a new leader.

The dawn **was breaking.**

NEGATIVE SENTENCES

He **was not eating** properly for quite some time.

He **was not meeting** anyone for a while.

He **was not riding** in the passenger's seat.

I **was not going** to jump farther or run faster.

INTERROGATIVE SENTENCES

Was the car **zooming** at a speed not permissible in the area?

Was he **contemplating** various options on this issue?

Was the nuclear reactor **functioning** well?

Was she **not facing** constant harassment?

Was she **not staying** on rent?

INTERROGATIVE SENTENCES [With Question Words]

Why **was** he **perspiring** in that bitter cold?

Why **was** he **struggling** to hold back tears?

4C. WAS + Being + Past Participle

"Past Continuous Tense – Passive Voice"

EXAMPLES:

AFFIRMATIVE SENTENCES

Freedom of expression **was being trampled**.

The plan **was being launched.**

A quiet notice **was being served**.

She **was being declared** elected.

The break-in **was being noticed.**

Traffic **was being stalled**.

NEGATIVE SENTENCES

Sub-standard material **was not being used** for the construction of the school building.

The tender **was not being scrapped**.

INTERROGATIVE SENTENCES

Was she **being operated on**?

Was the tent **not being erected**?

INTERROGATIVE SENTENCES [With Question Words]

Why **was** he **being evicted** from the hotel?

How **was** Independence Day **being celebrated?**

4D. WAS + Past Participle

"Past Indefinite Tense – Passive Voice"

EXAMPLES:

AFFIRMATIVE SENTENCES

A cup of coffee **was placed** in front of him.

A deal worth $30000 **was struck**.

A fake case **was slapped** against him.

A list of all schools which require repair **was prepared** by the education department.

A missile modified to "mimic" a hostile ballistic missile **was fired**.

A tearful farewell **was bid** to a slain police officer.

An AirAsia flight to Malaysia **was forced** back to Australia due to a technical problem.

Bird flu **was confirmed** in the state.

Consensus between the finance minister and the home minister **arrived**.

Their criticism **was driven** by "ulterior motives".

The crop **was hit** due to scanty rainfall.

The deadline for submitting the forms was **extended** to June 10.

The main gate **was illuminated** for the first time.

He lost consciousness after his car **was struck** by the train.

He said the ban **was put** in place.

He **was** allegedly **robbed** of ten thousand dollars.

He **was arrested** for being in possession of the arm.

He **was asked** to deposit $10,000 in three installments.

He **was charged** for holding assets beyond his known sources of income.

He **was dealt** a double blow.

He **was found** dead on the floor of his bedroom.

He **was greeted** by a crowd beating drums and shouting slogans.

He **was** last **heard** of on June 30 when he made a call to his family to inform them about his visit to the hill station.

He **was** later **booked** on charges of disturbing peace.

He **was left** with no will to live.

He **was saddened** by the latest corruption scandal.

He **was saved** by timely medical intervention.

They **were** so badly **beaten** that his ribs **were broken.**

His 60-minute speech **was punctuated** by a protest by some opposition members at certain points.

His life **was saved** because the doctors acted so promptly.

His marriage **was dissolved** by the high court.

His motorcycle **was parked** unlocked near a petrol pump.

His resignation **was accepted** *and* **forwarded** to the Governor.

I **was brought up** not to steal.

His victory **was announced** with drumbeats.

It **was torn** in two by the impact of the landing on a ground floor railing.

Lipstick, as we know it today, **was introduced** in England.

Moderate voting **was reported.**

National Security Act **was slapped** on him.

Normal life **was paralyzed** in response to the day-long shut down by the national party.

Our house **was illuminated** with bulbs.

His party **was placed** 4th in terms of percentage of total votes.

The power supply **was restored** soon after rectifying the glitch.

Printing of notes **was discontinued.**

The road **was re-carpeted**.

Security **was tightened**.

She **was exonerated** in a disproportionate assets case.

She **was** lovingly **called** 'Aunt'.

She **was lured** to Paris on the pretext of giving her a job.

She **was married** on Nov 27, 2000.

She **was seen** walking next to the leader.

She **was solemnized** by 'Qazi'.

The bag **was** safely **handed over** to the owner after verifying facts in the presence of an official of the department.

The center's decision to this effect **was conveyed** to CM.

The decision **was finalized** after hectic parleys till late on Friday.

The decline in growth **was witnessed** in almost all segments of the economy.

The earlier advisory **was misinterpreted**.

The good work done by the ruling party **was lost** to the public anger over the scam.

The initial lawsuit **was filed** against the two at-that-time unidentified officers.

The last time the staff strength **was increased** was in 1999.

The matter **was** eventually amicably **resolved** between the two sides

The road **was flanked** on one side by hills and on the other by a dam.

The ship **was broken** in two and **buried** deep in the sea-floor silt.

The shutdown call **was given** by the Bar association.

The young leopard **was found** resting inside the agricultural field of the village.

This strategy **was outlined** by none other than DIG.

The tiger **was untangled**.

Water **was filled** in her lungs.

Our contract **was canceled** without a fair hearing.

Work on this project **was started** four years ago.

<u>NEGATIVE</u> <u>SENTENCES</u>

The breakdown in the grid **was not** fully **corrected**.

The National Flag **was not hoisted** in an inverted position.

He **was not granted** an interest waiver.

A proper legal process **was not observed** in the trial.

He **was not implicated.**

He **was not shown** the courtesy and respect that he deserved as a head of state.

I **was not asked** for an explanation by the authorities.

He **was not seen** after he plunged into the river for a swim.

It **was not expected** of him.

She **was not born** into a wealthy family.

She **was not faced** with stiff resistance.

The dining area **was not cleaned** up after meals.

INTERROGATIVE SENTENCES

Was any business **transacted** in either house?

Was he **misunderstood** by the CM?

Was his condition **diagnosed** as swine flu?

Was the house also **damaged** by fire?

Was the power supply **hit** owing to broken wires and local faults?

Was she **met** with a flurry of verbal abuses?

Was the land fraudulently **sold** several times by one party to another?

Was the suspense **lifted**?

Was the work **not done** according to her instructions?

Was the wedding **not** quickly **solemnized**?

INTERROGATIVE SENTENCES [With Question Words]

Why **was** he **sacked?**

Why **was** the Cabinet **expanded?**

How **was** the London Underground **built?**

5A. English Grammar – 'Were'

English Verb 'WERE' Represents Past Events.

It Is Plural In a Sense.

It Is Used With 'You', 'We', 'They', and all 'Plural' Subjects.

EXAMPLES:

AFFIRMATIVE SENTENCES

All accused involved in the robbery **were** wanted criminals.

Authorities **were** too slow to distribute international aid that has flooded into the country.

Both the teams **were** equally strong.

Commuters **were** eager to travel and have a look at the first double-decker train on the route.

Doctors **were** available for first aid.

His actions **were** purely in the capacity of a journalist.

The limbs of the tiger, including its nails and teeth **were** intact.

The conditions **were** below any acceptable human standard.

The guns **were** silent the rest of the day.

They **were** all of the same family.

They **were** on foot.

They **were** rivals but decided to operate jointly in that matter.

Those talks **were** "propaganda to defame" me.

Thousands of people **were** in shelters.

Two planes **were** only one minute from colliding.

We **were** yet to verify the information.

NEGATIVE SENTENCES

Her joints **were not** stiff.

They **were not** on the wrong track.

INTERROGATIVE SENTENCES

Were his remarks in extremely bad taste?

Were they **not** lucky to win?

INTERROGATIVE SENTENCES [With Question Words]

Why **were** there bruises all over his body?

Why **were** they not careful?

5B. WERE + -ING Form of Verb

"Past Continuous Tense"

Expresses **-** Continued Action In the Past

EXAMPLES:

AFFIRMATIVE SENTENCES

Army engineers **were strengthening** weak spots on the banks of the river.

Constables **were demanding** a pay scale at par with employees from other departments.

Crops **were dying**.

Dancers **were tapping** their feet.

Doctors **were struggling** round the clock to tend to people with broken limbs, cracked skulls, ruptured flesh and worse.

Flies **were buzzing** around the whole place.

He regretted that authorities **were attempting** more to evade responsibility than mitigate the condition of workers.

Jail authorities **were deliberating** about various jobs that could be offered to prisoners.

Members of the family **were attending** a wedding at that time.

Most of them **were staring** at him.

My legs **were giving way** after I reached the finishing point.

Party leaders **were making** speeches.

Some youths **were gate-crashing** the wedding.

The floods **were receding.**

They **were blowing** conch shells.

They **were exchanging** hugs.

They **were speaking** to someone powerful and influential.

They **were taking** their routine early morning stroll when the accident happened.

Victims **were running out** of patience.

Villagers **were making** do with little food and a trickle of water.

We **were** only **doing** as were told.

We **were screening** the data in the pen drives and memory cards.

We **were sleeping** when suddenly the car alarm went off.

NEGATIVE SENTENCES

It has been found lately that some private hospitals **were not disposing of** their hazardous biomedical waste properly.

Passengers **were not creating** trouble.

INTERROGATIVE SENTENCES

Were four persons **traveling** in a utility vehicle used to transport goods?

Were people **crying** and **shouting**?

Were terrorists **mushrooming** here?

INTERROGATIVE SENTENCES [With Question Words]

Why **were** jets **flying** so low overnight yesterday?

Why **were** they **camping** in a forest?

How **were** you **feeling** last week?

5C. WERE + Being + Past Participle

"Past Continuous Tense – Passive Voice"

EXAMPLES:

AFFIRMATIVE SENTENCES

Acres of agricultural land **were being destroyed**.

Animals were crammed in a covered truck and **were being taken** to another state.

Answer sheets **were being corrected** by teachers having no knowledge of those subjects.

Efforts **were being made** to rectify the situation that has taken a bad shape.

Families **were being forced** to choose between mortgage and food.

More than a dozen boats **were being used** to search for about 100 people believed to be missing.

Operations **were being conducted** in makeshift OTs in tents.

Search-and-rescue teams **were being flown** in by helicopter.

Shops **were being reduced** to ashes.

Suspects **were being held** under anti-terrorism laws.

The blankets **were being distributed** to needy people.

They **were being questioned** yesterday.

They **were being rescued** alive.

They **were being treated** for gunshot wounds.

We **were being deplaned**.

When they were losing, the coaches **were being blamed.**

NEGATIVE SENTENCES

People **were not being suppressed**.

Things **were not being done** properly.

Windowpanes **were not being covered** with curtains.

INTERROGATIVE SENTENCES

Were food packets **being airdropped**?

Were students **not being offered** assistance by teachers?

INTERROGATIVE SENTENCES [With Question Words]

Why **were** we **being put** to the test?

Why **were** major projects **being scrapped**?

5D. WERE + Past Participle

"Past Indefinite Tense – Passive Voice"

EXAMPLES:

AFFIRMATIVE SENTENCES

300 electric poles **were uprooted** during the storm.

A majority of shop owners **were found** to be flouting the rules.

A series of dances **were performed** by the children of middle school from grades 2 to 4.

A truck hit us with great impact and we **were** all **thrown** on the road.

All roads leading to his house **were blocked** with cops frisking even media persons before allowing them entry.

Animals **were tied** by a rope to a pole allowing them to roam in a small area.

Big disparities **were alleged** between boys' and girls' sports.

Children **were buried** alive in the debris of their houses.

Counterfeit currencies of many countries having a face value of 1 million dollars **were seized**.

Dissenting voices **were outnumbered**.

Farmers **were told** to give thumb imprints.

Funds meant for the repair and restoration of the districts hit by the catastrophe **were misappropriated**.

It is a subject matter of investigation whether safety measures **were put** in place or not.

Machines **were installed** at the plant some ten months ago.

Major lapses **were uncovered.**

Many children **were forced** to assist their families to earn a decent income.

Many houses **were destroyed**.

Many local people said they **were denied** entry to the venue.

Mass cremations **were held** in the city.

Patients **were paralyzed** or otherwise harmed.

Pilgrims misjudged the river's depth and **were drowned**.

Roads to the length of 50 miles **were damaged**.

Roads **were swamped** by muck and debris from the mountain.

Senior cops **were seen** busy holding review meetings till late on Sunday.

Senior officials **were informed** of this problem but to no avail.

Seven deaths at a private nursing home **were investigated** by police.

Shutters of the dam **were lifted** with the water level reaching the maximum.

Ten rifles and five rocket launchers **were recovered** from militants.

Tens of houses **were buried** under a landslide.

The bombs **were synchronized** with a timer.

The city wore a cleaner and neater look after posters and hoardings **were removed.**

Their MRI examinations **were deemed** to be clinically necessary and **were performed** using a pre-specified safety protocol.

They **were found** in some bushes.

Trafficked victims **were rescued** from the factory.

Two students **were caught** cheating at two different examination centers.

Valuables **were found** intact with the body.

NEGATIVE SENTENCES

Reporting restrictions on the case **were not lifted**.

They **were not allowed** to vote in the election.

They **were not informed** about the cause of power outages.

Transfers **were not done** as per set norms and the tenure policy of bureaucrats.

We **were not given** a chance to explain our version.

INTERROGATIVE SENTENCES

Were clothes **found** hanging from trees?

Were damages or casualties **reported**?

Were students **booked** for the use of unfair means?

Were talks **delivered** on the greatness of Alfred Nobel?

Were they **confined** to a room for seven days?

Were they **seen** talking to each other?

Were they **served** poisoned food, leading to the death of all three?

Were tremors **felt** at multiple places across the city?

Were water supply and mobile connectivity **not disrupted** due to the storm?

INTERROGATIVE SENTENCES [With Question Words]

Why **were** your plans **rejected?**

How **were** the challenges **handled?**

How **were** you **treated** by your students?

Useful Notes (1): Question Tags

A tag question is a short question (e.g. aren't you? / are you?) that follows a statement.

In other words:

'Question tag' is a phrase such as - **isn't it?** Or **were they?** that you add to the end of a statement in order to turn it into a question or check that the statement is correct,

The pattern of Tag Question:

auxiliary verb + positive/negative meaning + pronoun of the subject + question mark (?)

In the negative tag question, we generally use the short form of not (i.e. **n't**) with the auxiliary verb.

A negative statement is followed by a positive tag question.

They **are not talking** about wedding plans, **are they**?

A positive statement is followed by a negative tag question.

They **are talking** about wedding plans, **aren't they**?

The tense of the tag is determined by the tense of the auxiliary verb of the statement that precedes it:

Democracy **is** much more than elections, **isn't it?**

He **isn't** a stress-free kind of guy, **is he**?

You **aren't** satisfied, **are you**?

He **was trying** to board the moving train, **wasn't he**?

She **wasn't forced** to flee from his village, **was she?**

They **were talking** about the goings-on in their office, **weren't they**?

When the statement contains a word with a negative meaning, the question tag needs to be positive.

Nothing is happening, **is it**?

NOTES:

01. Main sentence with the auxiliary verb 'Am':

Don't use **amn't** in the tag question. You should use **aren't.**

I **am** a simple person, **aren't I**?

02. Main sentence with the **subject 'this or that':**

Use the subject **'it'** on the question tag --

This is my computer, **isn't it?**

That is not my computer, **is it?**

03. Main sentence without subject and verb:

A horrific accident, **isn't it?**

In this sentence, 'Horrific accident' implies 'It is a horrific accident.'

04. Main Sentence with the subject 'there':

Use the subject **'there'** on the question tag –

There is a hero hidden in every one of us. **Isn't there**?

There isn't any pencil on the desk, **is there**?

There are many pens on the desk, **aren't there**?

There was an exchange of pleasantries, **wasn't there?**

There were cloudbursts, **weren't there?**

Important Note:

The meaning of the *question tag depends on how you say it. If the voice goes down, you are only asking for agreement or confirmation. If the voice goes up, you really want to know if the answer* is *yes or no.*

The Answer to Question Tags and Its Meaning

There are two possibilities for the answer to a question tag -- "yes" or "no".

The population **is growing** with every passing year, **isn't it**?

Yes, (=Population **is growing** with every passing year.) | **No** (=Population **is not growing** with every passing year.)

The population **is not growing** with every passing year, **is it**?

Yes, (=Population **is growing** with every passing year.) | **No** (=Population **is not growing** with every passing year.)

Useful Notes (2): Short Answers (Ellipsis]

AUXILIARY 'AM/IS/ARE/WAS/WERE' -- SHORT ANSWERS

Affirmative and negative short answers to questions –

Weren't you there?

Yes, I was. / No, I wasn't.

Wasn't she there?

Yes, she was. / No, she wasn't.

Pattern for Short Affirmative Answer --

Yes + pronoun + auxiliary 'am/is/are/was/were'

Pattern for Short Negative Answer --

No + pronoun + auxiliary 'am/is/are/was/were' + not (n't)

Example 1 --

Are you **planning** to cancel your tour?

Complete Affirmative Answer: **Yes,** I **am planning** to cancel my tour.

Short Affirmative answer: **Yes, I am.**

Complete Negative Answer: **No,** I **am not planning** to cancel my tour.

Short Negative answer: **No, I am not.**

Example 2 --

Is he hopeful that the scenario will change soon?

Complete Affirmative Answer: **Yes,** he **is** hopeful that the scenario will change soon.

Short Affirmative answer: **Yes, he is.**

Complete Negative Answer: **No,** he **isn't** hopeful that the scenario will change soon.

Short Negative answer: **No, he isn't.**

Example 3 --

Question: Are most people uncomfortable with the idea of eating alone at a restaurant?

Complete Affirmative Answer: **Yes,** most people **are** uncomfortable with the idea of eating alone at a restaurant.

Short Affirmative answer: **Yes, they are.**

Complete Negative Answer: **No,** most people **are not** uncomfortable with the idea of eating alone at a restaurant.

Short Negative answer: **No, they aren't.**

Example 4 --

Question: Was he **popping** balloons used for decoration?

Complete Affirmative Answer: **Yes,** he **was popping** balloons used for decoration.

Short Affirmative answer: **Yes, he was.**

Complete Negative Answer: **No,** he **was not popping** balloons used for decoration.

Short Negative answer: **No, he wasn't.**

Example 5 --

Question: Were they **ferrying** a sack of firecrackers on a bike?

Complete Affirmative Answer: **Yes,** they **were ferrying** a sack of firecrackers on a bike.

Short Affirmative answer: **Yes, they were.**

Complete Negative Answer: **No,** they **were not ferrying** a sack of firecrackers on a bike.

Short Negative answer: **No, they weren't.**

Useful Notes (3): Addition to Remarks

(A). Affirmative Addition to Affirmative Remarks

STRUCTURE

First Part: ***First Subject + Verb- 'Be + (Verb Participle / -ING Form of Verb) + Object or complement***

Connector: ***And or But***

Second Part: ***So + Verb- Be + Second Subject***

Second Part Could Be Re-written As Follows:

Subject + Verb- Be' + Also/Too

[Note – 'Subject' AND 'Verb' must agree with each other in the addition]

Example 1:

She **is watching** television, ***and so am*** I. *Or*

She **is watching** television, ***and*** I ***am too.***

Explanation:

She **is watching** television, ***and*** I ***am*** **watching** television ***too.***

Example 2:

I ***am*** part of a complex social system, ***and so are*** you. *Or*

I ***am*** part of a complex social system, ***and*** you ***are too.***

Explanation:

I ***am*** part of a complex social system, ***and*** you ***are*** part of a complex social system **too.**

Example 3:

The number of flu cases ***is*** on the rise, ***and so is*** the severity of the symptoms. *Or*

The number of flu cases ***is*** on the rise, ***and*** the severity of the symptoms ***is too.***

Explanation:

The number of flu cases ***is*** on the rise, ***and*** the severity of the symptoms ***is*** on the rise ***too.***

ADDITIONAL EXAMPLES –

Affirmative Addition to Affirmative Remarks -- Using 'So'

He ***is*** good at flying kites, ***and so am*** I.

They ***are*** confident of winning, ***but so am*** I.

He ***is*** an Olympic medal winner, ***and so am*** I.

You ***are*** crazy, ***and so am*** I.

Our world ***is*** constantly changing, ***and so are*** people.

We ***are*** serious business people, ***but so are*** they.

Fuel costs ***are going up***, ***and so are*** maintenance and engineering expenses.

She ***is focusing*** on doing what she does best, ***and so is*** everyone else.

Earnings ***are going up***, ***and so is*** the dividend.

He ***is*** a family person, **and so is** his wife.

My family ***is*** big, ***but so is*** his.

She ***was*** a competitive person, ***but so was*** I.

He ***is*** a very kind person, ***and so was*** his mom.

He ***was*** hit multiple times, ***and so was*** everyone else.

They ***were*** teary, ***and so was*** she.

Their backgrounds ***were*** diverse, ***and so were*** their skills.

He ***was*** Russian, ***and so were*** most of his acquaintances.

My whole family ***was*** here, ***and so were*** a lot of my friends.

The weeks ***were*** busy, ***and so were*** the weekends.

Addition to Remarks -- Using 'Too'

They ***are*** puzzled, ***and*** I ***am too.***

He ***is*** a fitness fanatic, ***and*** I ***am too.***

I ***am*** wordless, ***and*** he ***is too.***

I ***am*** on the phone ***and*** she ***is too.***

He ***is*** a deeply political person, ***and*** they ***are, too.***

She ***was*** optimistic about the future, ***and*** I ***was, too.***

He ***was*** happy with where things ***were, and*** we ***were too.***

(B). Negative Addition to Negative Remarks

STRUCTURE

***First Part:* First Subject + Verb- Be + Not + (Verb Participle / -ING Form of Verb) + Object or complement**

***Connector:* And**

***Second Part:* Neither (or Nor) + Verb- Be + Second Subject**

Second Part Could Be Re-written As Follows:

Second Subject + Verb- Be + Not + Either

[Note – 'Subject' AND 'Verb' must agree with each other in the addition]

Example 1:

She **is not listening** to music, ***and neither am*** *I. Or*

She **is not listening** to music, ***and*** I ***am not either.***

Explanation:

She **is not listening** to music, ***and*** I ***am not listening*** to music **either.**

Example 2:

I ***am not*** alone, ***and neither is*** anyone else. *Or*

I ***am not*** alone, ***and*** anyone else ***isn't either***.

Explanation:

I ***am not*** alone, ***and*** anyone else ***is not*** *alone* ***either.***

Example 3:

Public health ***is not*** just a local issue, ***and neither is*** climate change. *Or*

Public health ***is not*** just a local issue, ***and*** climate change ***isn't either***.

Explanation:

Public health ***is not*** just a local issue, ***and*** climate change ***isn't*** just a local issue ***either***.

ADDITIONAL EXAMPLES –

Negative Addition to Negative Remarks -- Using 'Neither'

You **are not** a nuclear scientist, ***and neither am*** I.

Nobody ***is*** perfect, ***and neither am*** I.

He ***is not going*** to make excuses, ***and neither am*** I.

She ***is not*** really temperamental, ***and neither am*** I.

You ***are not*** a mind reader — ***and neither is*** your partner!

Life ***is not*** fair, ***and neither is*** business!

I ***am not*** paid to have an opinion, ***and neither are*** you.

We ***are not going*** anywhere, ***and neither are*** you.

I ***am not*** a magician, ***and neither are*** they.

All migraines ***are not*** alike, ***and neither are*** the treatments.

She ***was not*** injured, ***and neither was*** her baby.

He ***was not*** happy with his career, ***and neither was*** his mother.

I ***was not*** born in Germany, ***and neither were*** my parents.

His stolen bag ***was not*** recovered, ***and neither were*** its contents.

Negative Addition to Negative Remarks -- Using 'Either'

You **are not** sure, and I **am not either.**

I **am not** a judgmental person, and she **isn't either.**

She **is not** a member of the wealthy elite, and you **aren't either.**

He **was not** ready to say goodbye, and I **wasn't either.**

In the beginning, they **were not** too serious about sports education, and we **weren't either.**

Useful Notes (4): There Is/Was and There Are/Were

"There is/was and There are/were + Noun" is used to indicate ***"to exist or to be present"***

When a sentence begins with there, the actual subject is considered to be the word/words following the verb. If the actual subject is singular in form, use a singular verb. If the actual subject is plural in form, use a plural verb.

Example (There Is):

There **is** normal activity across the state.

*[In this sentence, "actual subject" is **"activity"** which is singular in form so we used the singular verb **"is"** (in present tense)]*

Example (There Was):

There **was** a glow on his face.

*[In this sentence, "actual subject" is **"glow"** which is singular in form so we used the singular verb **"was"** (in past tense)]*

Example (There Are):

There **are** 30 children enrolled in our school.

*[In this sentence, "actual subject" is **"children"** which is plural in form so we used the plural verb **"are"** (in present tense)]*

Example (There Were):

There **were** reports of people scurrying for safety in several cities and towns.

*[In this sentence "actual subject" is **"reports"** which is plural in form so we used the plural verb **"were"** (in past tense)]*

More Examples [There Is]:

There **is** a persistent threat from his supporters.

There **is** a possibility of his expulsion from the organization.

There **is** a process to verify whether the idol is real or an imitation.

There **is** every possibility of it.

There **is** still a lot I can do.

There **is** a lot of work to do,

There **is** no case registered against him in the country.

There **is** something that we can learn from every human being.

There **is** some cheer for sugarcane farmers.

More Examples [There Are]:

There **are** over 40 buildings that are in shambles and might fall at any time.

There **are** people in society who can be set right only by severe punishments.

There **are** more things important in life than football!

There **are** very few complaints against them.

There **are** real consequences for fake threats.

There **are** ways to reduce flu risk.

There **are** endless stories like this.

There **are** various harmful cosmetic products available in the market that contain several low-quality ingredients and chemicals.

More Examples [There Was]:

There **was** an adverse environmental impact on the projects.

There **was** a division of votes.

There **was** more cheer for Brazil.

There **was** no need for her resignation.

There **was** a one-in-three likelihood of a rating downgrade for the country.

There **was** reportedly a heated argument between students and the police.

There **was** some panic because of the last year's situation.

There **was** something wrong with the quality of the meals.

There **was** the natural initial shock.

More Examples [There Were]:

There **were** 101 ***reasons***.

There **were** 50 ***complaints*** of staff misbehavior received by airlines.

There **were** economic ***hardships*** concerning the common man.

There **were** midnight ***knocks*** at my door.

There **were** ***reports*** of devastation in outlying, isolated mountainous areas after the 8-magnitude quake struck around noon.

INTERROGATIVE SENTENCES [Be + There]:

Is *there* any situation warranting the deployment of forces?

Is *there* any substance in the charge sheet?

Is *there* any surprise element in the outcome?

Was *there* a wedding scheduled in the family?

Was *there* a flood?

Was *there* dust everywhere outside the window?

Was *there* **not** a huge sound?

Was *there* **not** always a feeling of insecurity in his perusal life?

Was *there* provocation on behalf of the victims?

ALSO NOTE:

'HERE IS' (OR HERE'S) / 'HERE ARE' (OR HERE'RE)

'Here is' (or Here's) / 'Here are (or Here're)' is used to call attention to somebody/something present. It is also used for what the speaker possesses, brings, discovers, offers, etc.

Here is how your toothpaste may help fight malaria

Here is some more grim news.

Here is the expected petrol price for next month.

Here is the full list of golden globe winners.

Here is the ideal time to start saving for your retirement.

Here is the list of his career-best top 5 movies.

Here is what may shock the market this year

Here is what you need to know about the latest changes.

Here are the top 10 children's TV shows of all time.

Here are the top mutual funds that investors chose last year.

Useful Notes (5): Subjunctive Mood – 'Were'

'Subjunctive mood' is the verb (or form of a verb) that expresses ***wishes, uncertainty, unreality or hypothetical situation.*** The words **'if'** and **'wish'** usually indicate the subjunctive mood.

Past Subjunctive Mood is made up of the phrases "I were, He were, It were, etc."

The past and subjunctive conjugations of "to be":

Past tense of "to be":

I was / you were / he was / she was / it was / we were / they were

Subjunctive of "to be":

I were / you were / he were / she were / it were / we were / they were

Note:

Past Tense and Subjunctive Mood for the subject 'You, We, and They' are the same.

(A). Subjunctive Mood (Were) In Wishful Thinking (Wishes)

I ***wish*** my house **were** big. [You can't say: 'I wish my house was big']

Explanation:

I desire my house to be big. But my house is not big.

He ***wishes*** he **weren't** negligent. [You can't say: 'He wishes he wasn't negligent.']

Explanation:

He desires himself not to be negligent. But he is negligent.

Note:

Always use Subjunctive mood [were] with the word 'wish'.

The following phrases are always **wrong**:

I wish I was / I wish it was / he wishes he was / he wishes it was / she wishes she was / she wishes it was, etc.

(B). Subjunctive Mood (Were) In Hypothetical Situation

If he **were** honest, I ***would*** talk to him.

Explanation:

But he is not honest, so I have decided not to talk to him.

If she **were** fit, she ***would*** definitely join the meeting.

Explanation:

But she is not fit, so she is unable to attend the meeting.

NOTE:

"If I/he/she/it **was**" vs. "If I/he/she/it **were**"

"If I/he/she/it + **was**" indicates "unclear conditions" or "presumably true events in the past"

"If I/he/she/it + **were**" indicates "unreal or hypothetical events"

Examples:

If she **was** happy with her performance then it's OK.

[Presumably, she was happy with her performance.]

If she **were** happy with her performance, she would talk to me.

[But she is not happy with her performance]

(C). Subjunctive Mood (Were) In Unreal Statements

An old lady talked to me **as if** she **were** my mother.

Explanation:

But she was not my mother.

My friend scolds me **as though** he **were** a police officer.

Explanation:

But he is not a police officer.

Useful Notes (6): Be + Going To + Verb Word

"**Be + going to + Base Form of Verb**" implies:

(A). INTENTIONS/PLANS

[Used to express an idea in the near future]

I **am going to donate** my entire salary to the charity.

I **am going to do** it my way because that is what I think is right.

He **is going to fight** hard for his rights.

Are you **going to leave** your good job?

[This pattern is also used to express an idea that in the past you thought something would happen in the near future.]

He **was going to grow up** to be an architect.

I **was going to say** something to her, but I ended up not saying it.

(B). IMMINENT ACTIONS

Watch out! Somebody **is going to hit** you.

We **were going to get** everything he asked for.

(C). PREDICTION [USUALLY WITH CERTAINTY OR CONVICTION]

[Based on the evidence or experience you have.]

Nobody thinks I **am going to** win.

I can never gauge how well I **am going to do** in competition.

The fuel price **is going to rise** further.

Unchecked climate change **is going to be** stupendously expensive.

It **is going to rain.**

Global warming **is going to demolish** economies & societies.

None of these guys **are going to fight**.

I think we **are going to** qualify for the finals.

We knew it **was going to be** a tough game.

I knew it **was going to be** like this.

There **were going to be** many strikes and demonstrations by protestors.

If we didn't show up at the time we did, there **were going to be** serious consequences.

(D). COMMANDS OR OBLIGATION

[An employer to an employee] You **are going to correct** these errors right now.

GONNA

In informal English, you can use **"Gonna"** instead of **"Going To"**

We **are gonna be** a much better team. [=We are going to be a much better team.]

Note: "Be (Is/Am/Are) + Going to" is equivalent to **"Will"**

Useful Notes (7): 'Used to' Vs. 'Be + Used to'

"(Subject) + Used To + Base Form Of Verb" Vs. "(Subject) + Be + Used To + -Ing Form Of Verb"

"(Subject) + Used to + Verb Word" describes habits (repeated actions) or states in the past (which don't happen or exist in the present.)

I **used to *write*** a diary. [=But now I don't write a diary.]

He **used to *play*** hockey. [=But now he doesn't play hockey.]

She **used to *walk*** fast. [=But now she doesn't walk fast.]

They **used to *have*** a big house to live in. [=But now they don't have a big house to live in.]

"(**Subject) + Be + used to + -ING form of Verb**" describes an action that you are/were familiar with because you do/did or experience/experienced it often.

"Subject + Be + used to" is equivalent to "Subject + Be + Accustomed to"

I **am used to *writing*** a diary. [=I **am accustomed to** writing a diary.]

He **is used to *playing*** hockey. [=He **is accustomed to *playing*** hockey.]

We **are used to *working*** *hard*. [=We **are accustomed to *working*** *hard*.]

She **was used to *living*** *alone*. [=She **was accustomed to *living*** *alone*.]

They **were used to *walking*** fast. [=They **were accustomed to *walking*** fast.]

ADDITIONAL EXAMPLES:

(SUBJECT) + USED TO + BASE FORM OF VERB

I **used to study** for 7-8 hours a day without any depression and in a cool environment.

I **used to cook** for my grandma and grandpa when I was young.

I **used to deal** with money that numbered in the millions.

I **used to overdose** on vitamin C whenever my throat got a little scratchy.

My grandmother had a toy from her childhood that I **used to play** with.

I can never forget the days when I **used to roam** the streets of Washington.

He revealed that he **used to carry** a pistol wherever he used to travel.

He **used to be** great, but now he Is just good!

He **used to come** home from school and first finish her homework before going out to play.

He **used to follow** 400 accounts and now he only follows 40.

He **used to hang around** on the streets until 2 am.

He **used to say** he would die for the truth.

He **used to stammer** in his childhood.

He **used to tell** me some unbelievable stories

He **used to trade** on exchanges.

He **used to concentrate** on his work and didn't interact much with others.

He **used to work** at the air force base.

I **used to be** an introvert but find it easier to make friends now.

He **used to run** a garments business but it is all lost now.

He **used to write** poems since the age of seven and soon became famous.

He admitted that he **used to think** he was "the strangest boy in the world".

At the age of 10, she **used to shut** her eyes when speaking.

She **used to make** trips to attend concerts by her favorite artists.

She **used to purchase** most of her home appliances from the retailer.

She **used to put** herself through excessive exercise in an attempt to fit in.

She **used to seclude** himself for extended bouts of writing.

She **used to take care** of everything so that her daughter could just focus on her studies.

She **used to take** his children to the park to play on a Sunday morning.

When she was younger, she **used to pull** books off the shelves and look at the pictures.

As children, early in the morning, we **used to collect** wood for the bonfire.

We **used to play** golf, sometimes a couple of times a week.

We **used to bike** around town and **stop** and **talk** with people.

We **used to enjoy** setting firecrackers off.

We **used to earn** more than $25,000 a month.

We **used to hit** tennis balls the whole day.

Are video games less violent than they **used to be?**

I definitely see a trend where things are not like they **used to be.**

Obituaries are not what they **used to be.**

The jobs they **used to work** don't exist anymore.

They **used to be** able to feed their families and they can't feed their families now.

They **used to go** almost every Friday night to the skating rink.

They **used to live** near a nuclear plant.

We **used to watch** football all of the time.

(SUBJECT) + BE + USED TO + -ING FORM OF VERB

I **am used to meditating.**

I **am used to waking up** early.

I **am used to taking** on substantial risks in my investments.

I **am used to working** with them.

I **am used to getting** and **doing** what I want all the time.

As a retailer, I **am used to setting** my own hours and having holidays off or closing early.

I **am used to sharing** a close space with lots of different people.

I am a public intellectual and so I **am used to hearing** the wildest and most ignorant comments.

He **is used to singing** in public places.

As an actor, he **is used to performing** and **being** on stage.

She **is used to doing** my own laundry.

He **is used to sailing** fast boats,

As a hospital doctor, he **is used to working** under pressure,

She **is used to helping** other people.

She **is used to questioning** herself each time she makes a purchase.

She **is used to working** long hours in stressful work.

They **are used to fighting** for others.

We live close to the border so we **are used to seeing** soldiers around,

They **are used to working** in the darkness.

Players **are used to seeing** themselves on a big screen inside the stadium.

We **are used to being** online and **seeing** everybody giving their opinion on any and everything.

I **was used to doing** everything by myself.

I **was used to hearing** remarks about my weight.

They **were used to playing** in bad weather.

We **were used to serving** people and we **were used to solving** problems.

ALSO NOTE:

(Subject) + Be + used to + Noun [Equivalent to 'accustomed to']

He **is used to calls** from friends, friends of friends, relatives, friends of relatives and complete strangers.

Useful Notes (8): Be + To + Verb Word

"Be (Am/Is/Are) + to + Base form of Verb" is used to say what must or should be done. This pattern also implies somebody is supposed to do something; or something has been arranged, planned or organized for somebody (especially by somebody or something else.

Uses of **"Be (Am/Is/Are) + to + Base form of Verb"**

Responsibility or Obligation

She ***is to tell*** the whole truth. [= She is supposed to tell the truth]

I ***am to protect*** and care for my family.

The CEO of the company has announced he ***is to retire.***

The role of the mayor ***is to fulfill*** the wishes of the residents.

We ***are to make*** sure that we are doing things that help the country.

Arrangements (Official or Unofficial) In Advance

The tourism minister ***is to take*** part in an event here to promote the city as a tourism destination.

She ***is to have*** chemotherapy, starting with one session every three weeks.

They ***are to embark*** on a tour next year.

He ***is to undergo*** a medical examination on Friday.

Orders

You ***are to resign*** *as a non-executive director of the sports association right now.*

If + Subject + "Be (Am/Is/Are) + to + Base form of Verb"

This pattern is used to say that a particular aim can be achieved by doing a particular thing that is mentioned.

If we are to win the football tournament, we need to run a lot.

Infrastructure is an area where cities need increased investment ***if they are to meet*** the challenges of rapid urbanization.

We must unite ***if we are to have*** one voice and be heard,

NEGATIVE PATTERNS

"Be (Am/Is/Are) + not + to + Base form of Verb"

They ***are not to*** **blame** for the violence.

I ***am not to stay*** *silent.*

You ***are not to*** *question any decision made by me.*

You can also use the past form of **be (was and were)** *with* the ***"to + base form of the verb"***

I ***was to run*** *the race. [=I did run the race.]*

We ***were to save*** his life. *[=We did save his life.]*

You ***were not to join*** him on stage. *[=You, indeed, did not join him on stage.]*

Passive Voice of "Be (Am/Is/Are/Was/Were) + to + Base form of Verb"

"Be (Am/Is/Are/Was/Were) + to + 'Be' + Past Participle of Verb"

They ***are not to be trusted?***

He ***is to be suspended*** from the party for six years.

His plea ***was to be heard*** this morning in the court.

NOTE:

Difference Between ***"have/has/had + to"*** *and* ***"be (am/is/are/was/were) + to"—***

"have/has/had + to" implies a stronger form of obligation, compulsion or requirement than ***(am/is/are/was/were) + to"***

Useful Notes (9): Be + ‘Being”+ Adjective

He **is/was being *generous.*** Vs.
He **is/was *generous.***

"be + being + adjective" is used to emphasize the “limited period of time of particular action” of somebody.
You can use this pattern if somebody is/was behaving or acting in a way that is/was different from how they normally behave or act.

Difference between **"be + being + adjective”** and **"be + adjective"**
"be + being + adjective" implies a “limited period of time of particular action” or “deviation from the normal way of behaving/acting by somebody."
"be + adjective" implies the "permanent character" of somebody.

For example, if somebody is usually tight-fisted, but suddenly started doing charity then you can say:
He **is being *generous.***
For a past event, you can say:
He **was being *generous.*** [= He was behaving generously at that time.]

But if ‘generosity’ is the permanent character of somebody then you should say:
He **is *generous.***
To show the permanent character of ‘generosity’ in somebody in the past, you should say:
He **was *generous.***

However, there are some adjectives that are never used with "being". Especially, when the adjective refers to feelings, you should not use the continuous form.

For example, "happy, sad" can’t be used with "being". You can’t say:
I am being happy. [This is wrong]
You must say:
I am happy. [This is correct]

ADDITIONAL EXAMPLES ["be + being + adjective"]

I **am being** ***cautious*** about the rats in the room!

Am I **being** ***disloyal*** to him?

You **are being** ***disrespectful*** at this point.

Here, I **am being** quite an ***optimist.***

I **am being** ***respectful*** of cultural customs.

I **am being** ***imaginative***.

People say that I **am being** ***arrogant*** and I don't know how to deal with it.

I **am being** totally ***honest*** with you.

I enjoy myself when I **am being** ***productive.***

She **is being** very ***candid*** on this matter.

He **is being** as rigorous with himself as he is with other people.

He **is being** ***silly.***

Her mother **is being** too ***finicky*** about discipline.

You **are being** a little ***unfair*** to me.

You **are being** too ***judgmental***.

They **are being** ***greedy.***

Many actresses **are being *choosy*** with roles.

You **are being *selfish***.

I **was being *rude*** this morning.

I **was being *serious*** about quitting my job.

She told me once that I **was being *dismissive.***

He said I **was being *unsupportive*,** and that it was my duty to support him.

She felt like she **was being *deceitful*,** though it was never her intention.

I **was being *overconfident.***

I thought I **was being *diligent*,** yet they thought I **was being *rude.***

I knew I **was being *irritable*** but I couldn't get rid of it.

I **was being** too ***humble*** in my office.

Employees **were being *rebellious.***

They **were being *antisocial.***

She complained that they **were being *noisy.***

They **were being *hysterical.***

Also Note: "be + being + adjective + and + adjective"

I **am being *communicative*** *and* ***open.***

People have started to take more notice of him because he **is being *authentic*** *and* ***real.***

She **is being *inconsiderate*** *and* ***secretive.***

They **are being *careful*** *and* ***conscientious.***

He **was being *evil*** *and* ***dastardly*** to his rivals.

Useful Notes (10): Mixed Sentences

Mixed Sentences: Am/Is/Are/Was/Were

'Present Indefinite – Affirmative' + 'Present Continuous – Affirmative'

I **am** happy that he **is making** use of his talent for a good cause.

'Present Indefinite – Negative' + 'Present Continuous – Affirmative'

I **am not** of the opinion that these events **are happening** by chance.

'Present Continuous – Affirmative' + 'Present Indefinite – Affirmative'

Investigators **are** now **trying** to ascertain who made these forged documents and *whether* an organized gang **is** behind them.

The things they **are proposing** to do **are** a complete violation of users' privacy.

'Present Continuous – Affirmative' + 'Present Indefinite – Negative'

We **are trying** to look for anyone who **is not** here.

'Present Continuous – Affirmative (Passive)' + 'Present Indefinite – Affirmative'

Consumers **are being driven** by a sense that the worst **is** now over.

'Present Continuous – Affirmative (Passive)' + 'Present Continuous – Affirmative (Active)'

The city's garbage **is being dumped** in the open and it **is causing** large-scale pollution.

‘Past Continuous – Affirmative’ + ‘Past Perfect – Affirmative’

The vacation home they **were staying** in **was swept** away by rushing floodwaters.

‘Past Continuous – Affirmative and Negative forms’ in the same sentence

Some mysterious force **was telling** me that I **was not doing** the right thing.

‘Past Indefinite – Affirmative’ + ‘Past Perfect – Affirmative’

His hair **was** short and **was parted** to the left.

Most of his classmates **were** in the naughty category and **were punished** regularly.

‘Past Indefinite – Affirmative’ + ‘Present Indefinite – Affirmative’

It **was** and **is** an invitation.

‘Past Continuous – Affirmative (Passive)’ + ‘Past Indefinite – Affirmative’

I **was being blamed** for the fateful events of his life that **were** a product of his decisions and not mine.

‘Past Perfect – Affirmative’ + ‘Past Indefinite – Affirmative’

A woman **was seen** clutching her child, who **was** in tears.

‘Past Perfect – Affirmative and Negative forms’ in the same sentence

They **were given** time to correct code violations and **were not fined.**

Exercises: 1(A) and 1(B)

EXERCISE 1(A)

Fill in the blanks with "is" "am" and "are".

01. Both seats ___ likely to be picked up by him.

02. But to say nothing has been done ___ absolutely false.

03. Construction of the network of roads ___ bound to increase employment opportunities locally.

04. Dogs ___ hungrier in winter compared to the other seasons.

05. Drinking water ___ deficient.

06. Efforts ___ being made to provide a reliable and quality power supply.

07. Electricity lines in densely populated areas ___ causing a lot of trouble.

08. He ___ a dreamer wanting to fly like a bird.

09. He ___ being interviewed for the last two hours.

10. His killing ___ being treated as unexplained.

11. Houses ___ being given a thorough.

12. I ___ thankful for his warm welcome.

13. I know what kind of a person you ___.

14. It ___ a matter of concern and sorrow.

15. Once the beautification and renovation ___ done, the lake will be opened to tourists.

16. Rules of state spending ___ being reconsidered.

17. Sleeping too little ___ really bad for your health.

18. Some of the student groups ___ formed based on the interests of students.

19. That ___ the state of affairs.

20. The countdown for the launch of satellite ___ progressing smoothly.

21. The negligence of Municipal Corporation ___ resulted in the tress being harmed.

22. There ___ several cracks in the walls of the buildings.

23. There will be cases where pilots ___ being grounded.

24. They ___ finally see justice delivered.

25. We ___ all very worried.

ANSWERS TO THE EXERCISE 1(A):

1. are | 2. is | 3. is | 4. are | 5. is | 6. are | 7. are | 8. is | 9. is | 10. is | 11. are | 12. am | 13. are | 14. is | 15. is | 16. are | 17. is | 18. are | 19. is | 20. is | 21. is | 22. are | 23. are | 24. are | 25. are

EXERCISE 1(B)

Fill in the blanks with "was" or "were".

01. Car ___ rusting in the garage.

02. Carpeting of the road ___ completed.

03. Cars ___ lining up waiting to be searched at the checkpoint.

04. Driving through this stretch of bumpy road ___ a nightmare for commuters.

05. Essential services ___ exempted from the purview of the agitation.

06. Ground floor ___ rented out to a government department office.

07. He ___ extremely kind to me.

08. His eyes ___ being shut tight.

09. His speech ___ a ‘bundle of lies’ which lacked both intent and content.

10. In fact the opposite ___ true.

11. It ___ shocking that he ignored me.

12. Meeting ___ "positive, constructive and creative."

13. Security forces ___ marching on foot in the dirt track.

14. Streets ___ being strewn with rocks.

15. That ___ leading to unbearable stress among personnel.

16. The bedding ___ threadbare.

17. The court ___ not satisfied with the evidence produced by the investigating agency.

18. The crowd ___ boisterous and clapping.

19. The issue ___ being highlighted unnecessarily.

20. The tremors ___ so intense, like nothing we have ever experienced before.

21. There ___ some behind-the-scenes drama.

22. There ___ cobwebs in every corner of the ward.

23. Train services ___ halted for a short duration.

24. Two teams ___ raiding his likely hideouts and residences.

25. Water supply and mobile connectivity ___ also disrupted due to the storm.

ANSWERS TO THE EXERCISE 1(B):

1. was | 2. was | 3. were | 4. was | 5. were | 6. was | 7. was | 8. were | 9. was | 10. was | 11. was | 12. was | 13. were | 14. were | 15. was | 16. was | 17. was | 18. was | 19. was | 20. were | 21. was | 22. were | 23. were | 24. were | 25. was

Exercises: 2(A) to 2(E)

EXERCISE 2(A) -- (Verb 'to be' – 'AM')

Rewrite the following sentences in the correct word order:

WRONG WORD ORDER

1. I am story afraid to tell not anymore my.
2. I am you to here not impress.
3. I am and everything alert curious, open, to.
4. I am principles for stand ready to my.
5. I am artist not a, but now born it comes to me naturally.
6. I am for all the evil they sorry done have against you.
7. I am airport on way the to.
8. I am and a skill believer great in intrinsic talent.
9. I am being with my office helped work.
10. I am considered to person be a sincere.

ANSWERS TO THE EXERCISE 2(A) [CORRECT WORD ORDER]

1. I **am not** afraid to tell my story anymore.
2. I **am not** here to impress you.
3. I **am** curious, open, and alert to everything.
4. I **am** ready to stand for my principles.
5. I **am not** a born artist, but now it comes to me naturally.
6. I **am** sorry for all the evil they have done against you.
7. I **am** on the way to the airport.
8. I **am** a great believer in intrinsic skill and talent.
9. I **am being helped** with my office work.
10. I **am considered** to be a sincere person.

EXERCISE 2(B) -- (Verb 'to be' – 'IS')

Rewrite the following sentences in the correct word order:

WRONG WORD ORDER

1. He desperate is to resolve the dispute.
2. There space interest great deal a of is new in.
3. Public eroding faith political is in the class fast.
4. Their selling main source is of income milk.
5. Artificial making role intelligence is investment taking on a bigger in decisions.
6. More collected being is terror information on the attack.
7. The residents jointly owned shop by is two local.
8. The trust is in headquartered Tokyo.
9. Is plastic live possible to without it?
10. Our housed school being library in two big is rooms.

ANSWERS TO THE EXERCISE 2(B) [CORRECT WORD ORDER]

1. He **is** desperate to resolve the dispute.
2. There **is** a great deal of new interest in space.
3. Public faith in the political class **is** fast **eroding**.
4. Their main source of income **is selling** milk.
5. Artificial intelligence **is taking** on a bigger role in making investment decisions.
6. More information **is being collected** on the terror attack.
7. The shop **is** jointly **owned** by two local residents.
8. The trust **is headquartered** in Tokyo.
9. **Is** it possible to live without plastic?
10. Our school library **is being housed** in two big rooms.

EXERCISE 2(C) -- (Verb 'to be' – 'ARE')

Rewrite the following sentences in the correct word order:

WRONG WORD ORDER

1. Fake are emails harmful to your finances.
2. Actions akin and effect their outcomes to the cause and are principle.
3. They education are disrupting and health care.
4. Threats to peace lurking in the are border.
5. Memories of being the past are brought to life through writing.
6. Results are of preference votes being announced.
7. Are leading stress anxiety not the and of sickness in the causes workforce?
8. Consequences being paddy of prices felt are by declining farmers.
9. More finishing are and more elementary children school.
10. Index investment establishing firms looking into are funds for cryptocurrencies.

ANSWERS TO THE EXERCISE 2(C) [CORRECT WORD ORDER]

1. Fake emails **are** harmful to your finances.
2. Actions and their outcomes **are** akin to the cause-and-effect principle.
3. They **are disrupting** education and health care.
4. Threats to peace **are lurking** at the border.
5. Memories of the past **are being brought** to life through writing.
6. Results of preference votes **are being announced**.
7. **Are** stress and anxiety **not** the leading causes of sickness in the workforce?
8. The consequences of declining paddy prices **are being felt** by farmers.
9. More and more children **are finishing** elementary school.
10. Investment firms **are looking** into establishing index funds for cryptocurrencies.

EXERCISE 2(D) -- (Verb 'to be' – 'WAS')

Rewrite the following sentences in the correct word order:

WRONG WORD ORDER

1. The city grip in the of was a full-blown riot.
2. The police was chief behaving like a tyrant in a democratic setup.
3. A blood was being camp organized donation.
4. A was planned search operation carried out.
5. He a bulldozer on was a farm was and realized driving something wrong.
6. She rescued submarine at sea after was his day sank the same.
7. Education conducting board with the work of was five exams overburdened simultaneously.
8. I for an interview was by called the given selection committee and the job.
9. A bank shepherd was his goats herding near the river.
10. She committed was fearless and supporting the to people.

ANSWERS TO THE EXERCISE 2(D) [CORRECT WORD ORDER]

1. The city **was** in the grip of a full-blown riot.
2. The police chief **was behaving** like a tyrant in a democratic setup.
3. A blood donation camp **was being organized**.
4. A planned search operation **was carried** out.
5. He **was driving** a bulldozer on a farm and realized something **was** wrong.
6. She **was** rescued at sea after his submarine sank the same day.
7. The education board **was overburdened** with the work of conducting five exams simultaneously.
8. I **was called** for an interview by the selection committee and **given** the job.
9. A shepherd **was herding** his goats near the river bank.
10. She **was** fearless and committed to supporting the people.

EXERCISE 2(E) -- (Verb 'to be' – 'WERE')

Rewrite the following sentences in the correct word order:

WRONG WORD ORDER

1. They when office queuing came outside I to were open the.
2. There no roads connecting the were village to the main town.
3. Furnace units running at were half of their capacities.
4. Officials from said they field busy collecting data the were level staff.
5. They being treated were for facial injuries.
6. Workers were forced into the union being illegally.
7. All were parameters of the test firing met.
8. Most players on were of the 10 probably each of the two teams juniors.
9. We noticed surprised many that so were people us.
10. There falls of snow in the town were heavy yesterday, were where the closed vast majority of schools.

ANSWERS TO THE EXERCISE 2(E) [CORRECT WORD ORDER]

1. They **were queuing** outside when I came to open the office.
2. There **were** no roads connecting the village to the main town.
3. Furnace units **were running** at half of their capacities.
4. Officials said they **were** busy collecting data from the field-level staff.
5. They **were being tre**ated for facial injuries.
6. Workers **were being forced** into the union illegally.
7. All parameters of the test firing **were met**.
8. Most of the 10 players on each of the two teams **were** probably juniors
9. We **were surprised** that so many people noticed us.
10. There **were** heavy falls of snow in the town yesterday, where the vast majority of schools **were closed.**

****

About the Author

Manik Joshi was born on January 26, 1979, at Ranikhet, a picturesque town in the Kumaon region of the Indian state of Uttarakhand. He is a permanent resident of the Sheeshmahal area of Kathgodam located in the city of Haldwani in the Kumaon region of Uttarakhand in India. He completed his schooling in four different schools. He is a science graduate in the ZBC – zoology, botany, and chemistry – subjects. He is also an MBA with a specialization in marketing. Additionally, he holds diplomas in "computer applications", "multimedia and web-designing", and "computer hardware and networking". During his schooldays, he wanted to enter the field of medical science; however, after graduation, he shifted his focus to the field of management. After obtaining his MBA, he enrolled in a computer education center; he became so fascinated with working on the computer that he decided to develop his career in this field. Over the following years, he worked at some computer-related full-time jobs. Following that, he became interested in Internet Marketing, particularly in domaining (business of buying and selling domain names), web design (creating websites), and various other online jobs. However, later he shifted his focus solely to self-publishing. Manik is a nature-lover. He has always been fascinated by overcast skies. He is passionate about traveling and enjoys solo travel most of the time rather than traveling in groups. He is actually quite a loner who prefers to do his own thing. He likes to listen to music, particularly when he is working on the computer. Reading and writing are definitely his favorite pastimes, but he has no interest in sports. Manik has always dreamed of a prosperous life and prefers to live a life of luxury. He has a keen interest in politics because he believes it is politics that decides everything else. He feels a sense of gratification sharing his experiences and knowledge with the outside world. However, he is an introvert by nature and thus gives prominence to only a few people in his personal life. He is not a spiritual man, yet he actively seeks knowledge about the metaphysical world; he is particularly interested in learning about life beyond death. In addition to writing academic/informational text and fictional content, he also maintains a personal diary. He has always had a desire to stand out from the crowd. He does not believe in treading the beaten path and avoids copying someone else's path to success. Two things he always refrains from are smoking and drinking; he is a teetotaler and very health-conscious. He usually wakes up before the sun rises. He starts his morning with meditation and exercise. Fitness is an integral and indispensable part of his life. He gets energized by solving complex problems. He loves himself the way he is and he loves the way he looks. He doesn't believe in following fashion trends. He dresses according to what suits him & what he is comfortable in. He believes in taking calculated risks. His philosophy is to expect the best but prepare for the worst. According to him, you can't succeed if you are unwilling to fail. For Manik, life is about learning from mistakes and figuring out how to move forward.

Amazon Author Page of Manik Joshi:
https://www.amazon.com/author/manikjoshi

Email: manik85joshi@gmail.com

BIBLIOGRAPHY

(A). SERIES TITLE: "ENGLISH DAILY USE" *[40 BOOKS]*

01. How to Start a Sentence
02. English Interrogative Sentences
03. English Imperative Sentences
04. Negative Forms In English
05. Learn English Exclamations
06. English Causative Sentences
07. English Conditional Sentences
08. Creating Long Sentences In English
09. How to Use Numbers In Conversation
10. Making Comparisons In English
11. Examples of English Correlatives
12. Interchange of Active and Passive Voice
13. Repetition of Words
14. Remarks In the English Language
15. Using Tenses In English
16. English Grammar- Am, Is, Are, Was, Were
17. English Grammar- Do, Does, Did
18. English Grammar- Have, Has, Had
19. English Grammar- Be and Have
20. English Modal Auxiliary Verbs
21. Direct and Indirect Speech
22. Get- Popular English Verb
23. Ending Sentences with Prepositions
24. Popular Sentences In English
25. Common English Sentences
26. Daily Use English Sentences
27. Speak English Sentences Every Day
28. Popular English Idioms and Phrases
29. Common English Phrases
30. Daily English- Important Notes
31. Collocations In the English Language
32. Words That Act as Multiple Parts of Speech (Part 1)
33. Words That Act as Multiple Parts of Speech (Part 2)
34. Nouns In the English Language
35. Regular and Irregular Verbs
36. Transitive and Intransitive Verbs

37. 10,000 Useful Adjectives In English
38. 4,000 Useful Adverbs In English
39. 20 Categories of Transitional Expressions
40. How to End a Sentence

****

<u>(B).</u> <u>SERIES TITLE:</u> <u>“ENGLISH WORD POWER”</u> <u>*[30 BOOKS]*</u>

01. Dictionary of English Synonyms
02. Dictionary of English Antonyms
03. Homonyms, Homophones and Homographs
04. Dictionary of English Capitonyms
05. Dictionary of Prefixes and Suffixes
06. Dictionary of Combining Forms
07. Dictionary of Literary Words
08. Dictionary of Old-fashioned Words
09. Dictionary of Humorous Words
10. Compound Words In English
11. Dictionary of Informal Words
12. Dictionary of Category Words
13. Dictionary of One-word Substitution
14. Hypernyms and Hyponyms
15. Holonyms and Meronyms
16. Oronym Words In English
17. Dictionary of Root Words
18. Dictionary of English Idioms
19. Dictionary of Phrasal Verbs
20. Dictionary of Difficult Words
21. Dictionary of Verbs
22. Dictionary of Adjectives
23. Dictionary of Adverbs
24. Dictionary of Formal Words
25. Dictionary of Technical Words
26. Dictionary of Foreign Words
27. Dictionary of Approving & Disapproving Words
28. Dictionary of Slang Words
29. Advanced English Phrases
30. Words In the English Language

****

(C). SERIES TITLE: "WORDS IN COMMON USAGE" *[10 BOOKS]*

01. How to Use the Word "Break" In English
02. How to Use the Word "Come" In English
03. How to Use the Word "Go" In English
04. How to Use the Word "Have" In English
05. How to Use the Word "Make" In English
06. How to Use the Word "Put" In English
07. How to Use the Word "Run" In English
08. How to Use the Word "Set" In English
09. How to Use the Word "Take" In English
10. How to Use the Word "Turn" In English

****

(D). SERIES TITLE: "WORDS BY NUMBER OF LETTERS" *[10 BOOKS]*

01. Dictionary of 4-Letter Words
02. Dictionary of 5-Letter Words
03. Dictionary of 6-Letter Words
04. Dictionary of 7-Letter Words
05. Dictionary of 8-Letter Words
06. Dictionary of 9-Letter Words
07. Dictionary of 10-Letter Words
08. Dictionary of 11-Letter Words
09. Dictionary of 12- to 14-Letter Words
10. Dictionary of 15- to 18-Letter Words

****

(E). SERIES TITLE: "ENGLISH WORKSHEETS" *[10 BOOKS]*

01. English Word Exercises (Part 1)
02. English Word Exercises (Part 2)
03. English Word Exercises (Part 3)
04. English Sentence Exercises (Part 1)
05. English Sentence Exercises (Part 2)
06. English Sentence Exercises (Part 3)
07. Test Your English
08. Match the Two Parts of the Words
09. Letter-Order In Words
10. Choose the Correct Spelling

Printed in Great Britain
by Amazon

56152905R00057